About This Book

Title: *Sweet Treats*

Step: 5

Word Count: 201

Skills in Focus: Long vowel e spelled ee and ea

Tricky Words: after, another, forest, cherry, lemon, pink, put

Ideas For Using This Book

Before Reading:
- **Comprehension:** Look at the title and cover image together. Walk through the pictures in the book with readers and have them make predictions about what they might learn in the book. Help them make connections by asking what they already know about desserts around the world.
- **Accuracy:** Practice saying the tricky words listed on page 1.
- **Phonics:** Tell students they will read words with the long vowel teams *ea* and *ee*. Explain that *ee* and *ea* both make the long vowel sound /e/. Have students look at the title of this book, *Sweet Treats*. Ask readers to point to the vowel pairings in each word of the title. Help them practice blending the sounds in the words. Have students take a quick walk through the first few pages of text to identify and decode additional long vowel *e* words.

During Reading:
- Have readers point under each word as they read it.
- **Decoding:** If readers are stuck on a word, help them say each sound and blend the sounds together smoothly. Be sure to point out words with *ee* and *ea* as they appear.
- **Comprehension:** Invite readers to talk about new things they are learning about desserts around the world while reading. What are they learning that they didn't know before?

After Reading:
Discuss the book. Some ideas for questions:
- What are some kinds of desserts around the world?
- What desserts have you had before? What new desserts would you like to try?

Sweet Treats

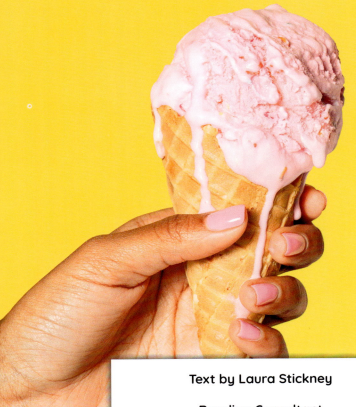

Text by Laura Stickney

Reading Consultant
Deborah MacPhee, PhD
Professor, School of Teaching and Learning
Illinois State University

PICTURE WINDOW BOOKS
a capstone imprint

It is fun to eat sweet treats. You eat them after meals.

You can get treats in lots of places.

You can get ice cream as a treat.

It can be green, pink, or blue.

Scoop it in a cone and lick it.

Scoop ice cream in a mug and put root beer on it.

Then it is a root beer float.
Eat it with a spoon.

Ice cream melts in the heat. Eat it fast!

But watch out
for brain freeze!

You can eat treats made with seeds, rice, and dates.

You can eat sweet buns made with red bean paste.

Sweet buns are sticky snacks.

You can drink tea with these treats.

17

Another sweet treat is Black Forest cake. It is rich. It is made with real cherry jam.

You can eat flan.

This treat is made with eggs and sweet milk.

To make flan, crack eggs.

Then you need to beat the eggs.

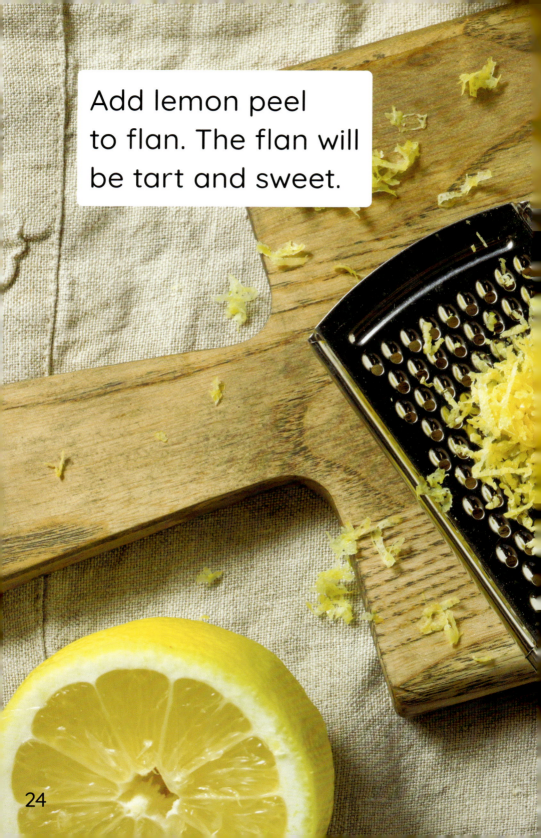

Add lemon peel to flan. The flan will be tart and sweet.

In Chad, you can eat a treat that is like oatmeal.

This treat is made with rice, wheat, and peanuts.

Let's make lots of neat treats. Each treat is a dream to eat!

More Ideas:

Phonics Activity

Read the Room with *ea* and *ee*:
Prepare word cards with *ea* and *ee* words. Place them around the classroom or workspace. Provide a sheet of paper labeled with the target spelling patterns *ea* and *ee* in a two-column format. Have readers walk around the room to locate each word card, read the word, and then write the word under the correct vowel team.

Suggested words:

ea: each, treat, eat, meals, cream, heat, dream, real, tea, beat, bean, neat

ee: sweet, green, need, peel, feels, seeds

Extended Learning Activity

Draw a Dessert:
Ask readers to draw an ice cream sundae. Have them start by drawing a dish or bowl. Then have them add scoops of ice cream and toppings to the drawing. For each scoop or topping they draw, have readers write down a sentence describing it. Challenge readers to use words with *ea* or *ee* vowel teams.

Published by Picture Window Books, an imprint of Capstone
1710 Roe Crest Drive, North Mankato, Minnesota 56003
capstonepub.com

Copyright © 2026 by Capstone.
All rights reserved. No part of this publication may be reproduced in whole or in part, or stored in a retrieval system, or transmitted in any form or by any means, electronic, mechanical, photocopying, recording, or otherwise, without written permission of the publisher.

Library of Congress Cataloging-in-Publication Data is available on the Library of Congress website.

ISBN: 9798875227165 (hardback)
ISBN: 9798875230714 (paperback)
ISBN: 9798875230691 (eBook PDF)

Image Credits: iStock: bhofack2, 24-25, Liudmila Chernetska, 1, 20-21, mvp64, 10-11, Prostock-Studio, 4-5, Rian Maulana, cover, Veliavik, 12-13; Red Line Editorial: 9, 13, 15, 17, 19, 21, 27; Shutterstock: Anna Shepulova, 16-17, Brent Hofacker, 8-9, Fanfo, 26-27, irina2511, 18-19, masa44, 14-15, Prostock-Studio, 30, Rawpixel.com, 3, ShineTerra, 6-7, Vitawin, 28-29, Wita Design, 22-23, 32

Printed and bound in Malaysia.   6274